LET'S WORK IT OUT

How to deal with FIGHTING

Jonathan Kravetz

PowerKiDS press

New York

Published in 2007 by The Rosen Publishing Group, Inc.
29 East 21st Street, New York, NY 10010

First Edition

Editor: Jennifer Way
Book Design: Ginny Chu
Layout Design: Kate Laczynski
Photo Researcher: Sam Cha

Photo Credits: Cover, p. 1 © The Image Works, Inc.; pp. 4, 18 © Index Stock Imagery, Inc.; p. 6 © SuperStock, Inc.; pp. 8, 20 © www.istockphoto.com; p. 10 © The Image State; pp. 12, 14, 16 © Corbis.

Library of Congress Cataloging-in-Publication Data

Kravetz, Jonathan.
    How to deal with fighting / Jonathan Kravetz. — 1st ed.
        p. cm. — (Let's work it out)
    Includes index.
    ISBN-13: 978-1-4042-3672-1 (lib. bdg.)
    ISBN-10: 1-4042-3672-4 (lib. bdg.)
    1. Aggressiveness in children—Juvenile literature. I. Title.
    BF723.A35K73 2007
    303.6'9—dc22
                                    2006027112

Manufactured in the United States of America

Contents

People have disagreements sometimes, and that is OK.
It is important not to let a disagreement turn into a fight.

Fights

Everyone disagrees sometimes. If two people are watching the same TV, maybe one wants to watch a game show and another wants to watch sports. This is a disagreement. You might want to play with a game at school. Someone else wants it, too. This is also a disagreement.

Sometimes when people cannot work out their disagreements, they fight. No one really wins in a fight, though. In this book we will learn about fighting and how to deal with it.

Horseplay can get out of hand and turn into a fight if one person gets hurt and becomes angry.

How Fights Start

Imagine one person is making fun of another person. Both kids might become angry. The two kids begin an **argument**. Soon both of them lose control of their anger and start fighting.

People often begin fights when they lose control of their anger during an argument. Fights may also start when someone gets pushed or hit. Fights can start when people are horseplaying. One person might hurt the other person by mistake and make him or her angry. Fights can also happen when people say mean things to each other. Some children like to fight. They are called bullies.

People often do not listen to each other when they are having a verbal fight.

Fighting with Words

When people disagree with each other, it does not always mean they are fighting. Talking is the best way to work out a disagreement. By talking it out and listening to each other, people can **calmly** tell each other how they feel.

When people start yelling, screaming, and saying mean things, they are no longer working out their problems. No one is listening to what the other person is saying. When they argue this way, they are fighting with words. This is called **verbal** fighting. Fighting this way does not help **solve** disagreements. It makes people angrier.

During a physical fight, people can lose control and get hurt or hurt the other person.

Physical Fights

A fight can start over something simple, such as a toy that two people want to play with but do not want to share. They might start arguing, but soon both of them lose control of their anger and start hitting each other. This is an example of a verbal fight turning into a **physical** fight.

In physical fights people might hit, kick, pull hair, or bite. People often get hurt during physical fights. Physical fighting is not a good way to solve problems. Getting into fights only makes the problem worse.

People pick fights for many reasons. You may be scared, or you may want to fight. The best thing to do, though, is to walk away.

If Someone Picks a Fight

There are many reasons other kids might pick a fight with you. They might suffer from **low self-esteem**. By picking on others and making them feel bad, they hope to make themselves feel better. They might want attention, or they cannot control their anger.

If someone picks a fight with you, the best thing to do is to tell that person you do not want to fight. Walk away after that. If someone hurts you, tell an adult whom you trust.

There are other, more positive, ways to solve your problems than by getting into fights.

If You Are Starting Fights

If you are getting into trouble for fighting, then you are hurting others. You are not solving any problems that you might have with other people. You need to learn ways to control your anger so that you can stop getting into fights.

You might try walking away before you get angry. You might also talk to a calm person. You can also try to talk calmly with the person with whom you are angry. This can lead to **compromise**. Before you start a fight, think about what will happen.

Staying calm can help you think clearly. This can help you find good ways to work through problems.

Staying Calm

A good way to keep from getting into fights is to stay calm during disagreements. Staying calm will help you listen to what others are saying. When people are not calm, they do not listen well.

Before getting into a fight, think about how much better off you will be if you stay calm. When you start to feel angry, tell yourself to stay calm. You can do this by taking deep breaths and counting to 10. Keeping a cool head will help you work out a problem and help keep you from starting a fight.

When people show respect for one another's feelings,
it is easier for them to work through disagreements.
Even good friends disagree sometimes.

Talking It Out

The best way to **resolve** a disagreement is to talk it out. That means you must also listen to each other. Talk about the problem and how it might be fixed.

When you talk it out, try to think of a **solution** that will give both sides something. Try to understand the other person's way of thinking. Always show respect for the other person's feelings. When people learn to compromise, they are much happier with the solutions to disagreements.

Sometimes it can help to talk to adults about your feelings and fears. They might help you find solutions to your problems.

Getting Help

Sometimes it will make sense to get a person who is not a part of the disagreement to help you solve your problem. A parent, teacher, or other friend can help come up with a fair solution everyone can agree on. This can help keep a fight from starting.

If you feel really afraid or you think you might be in danger, do not try to solve the problem yourself. Find an adult you can trust and talk about your fears.

No More Fighting

Once you have learned to deal with **conflict** without fighting, you will find it easier to make and keep friends. You will stay calm and out of trouble.

Remember that you have more than one **choice** you can make when faced with a disagreement. You can walk away. You can also stay calm and talk out the problem. You can even ask another person to help you with the disagreement. These are all good ways to work out a problem without getting into a fight.

Glossary

argument (AR-gyoo-mint) A disagreement.

calmly (KAHM-lee) In a manner that is not angry.

choice (CHOYS) The act of picking.

compromise (KOM-pruh-myz) To give up something to reach an agreement.

conflict (KON-flikt) A fight or a struggle.

low self-esteem (LOH self-uh-STEEM) Not having pride or respect for yourself. Children with low self-esteem feel people are always judging them.

physical (FIH-zih-kul) Having to do with the body.

resolve (rih-ZOLV) To decide.

solution (suh-LOO-shun) An answer to a problem.

solve (SOLV) To figure something out.

verbal (VER-bul) With words.

23

Index

Web Sites

Due to the changing nature of Internet links, PowerKids Press has developed an online list of Web sites related to the subject of this book. This site is updated regularly. Please use this link to access the list:

www.powerkidslinks.com/lwio/fight/